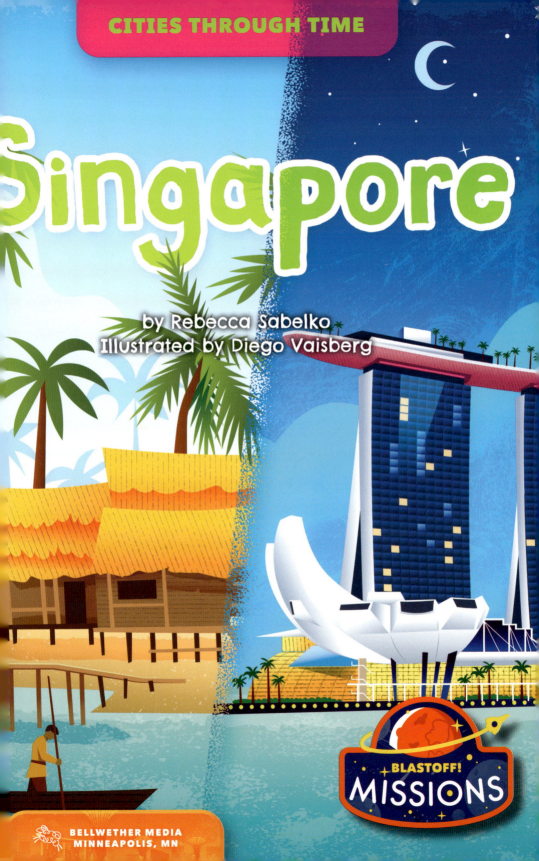

Blastoff! Missions takes you on a learning adventure! Colorful illustrations and exciting narratives highlight cool facts about our world and beyond. Read the mission goals and follow the narrative to gain knowledge, build reading skills, and have fun!

Traditional Nonfiction

Narrative Nonfiction

Blastoff! Universe

MISSION GOALS

> FIND YOUR SIGHT WORDS IN THE BOOK.

> LEARN ABOUT IMPORTANT EVENTS IN SINGAPORE'S HISTORY.

> LEARN HOW SINGAPORE BECAME A MODERN CITY-STATE.

This edition first published in 2025 by Bellwether Media, Inc.

No part of this publication may be reproduced in whole or in part without written permission of the publisher. For information regarding permission, write to Bellwether Media, Inc., Attention: Permissions Department, 6012 Blue Circle Drive, Minnetonka, MN 55343.

Library of Congress Cataloging-in-Publication Data

Names: Sabelko, Rebecca, author.
Title: Singapore / by Rebecca Sabelko.
Description: Minneapolis, MN : Bellwether Media Inc., 2025. | Series: Blastoff! Missions : cities through time | Includes bibliographical references and index. | Audience: Ages 5-8 | Audience: Grades 2-3 | Summary: "Vibrant illustrations accompany information about the history of Singapore. The narrative nonfiction text is intended for students in kindergarten through third grade" -- Provided by publisher.
Identifiers: LCCN 2024021454 (print) | LCCN 2024021455 (ebook) | ISBN 9798886870039 (library binding) | ISBN 9798893041415 (paperback) | ISBN 9781644878408 (ebook)
Subjects: LCSH: Singapore--Juvenile literature.
Classification: LCC DS609 .S33 2025 (print) | LCC DS609 (ebook) | DDC 959.57--dc23/eng/20240604
LC record available at https://lccn.loc.gov/2024021454
LC ebook record available at https://lccn.loc.gov/2024021455

Text copyright © 2025 by Bellwether Media, Inc. BLASTOFF! MISSIONS and associated logos are trademarks and/or registered trademarks of Bellwether Media, Inc. Bellwether Media is a division of Chrysalis Education Group.

Editor: Christina Leaf   Designer: Laura Sowers

Printed in the United States of America, North Mankato, MN.

This is **Blastoff Jimmy!** He is here to help you on your mission and share fun facts along the way!

Table of Contents

Welcome to Singapore!	4
A City by the Sea	6
A Modern City	16
The City Today	20
Glossary	22
To Learn More	23
Beyond the Mission	24
Index	24

Welcome to Singapore!

Singapore is a busy place! Nearly 6 million people live in this small **city-state**. Visitors walk through gardens. People check out shops.

Let's learn how Singapore became what it is today!

A City by the Sea

1200s

Off the shore of Temasek, Orang Laut people are **foraging** and fishing. They collect plants in the **mangroves** and catch fish.

The sea is important to their **culture**!

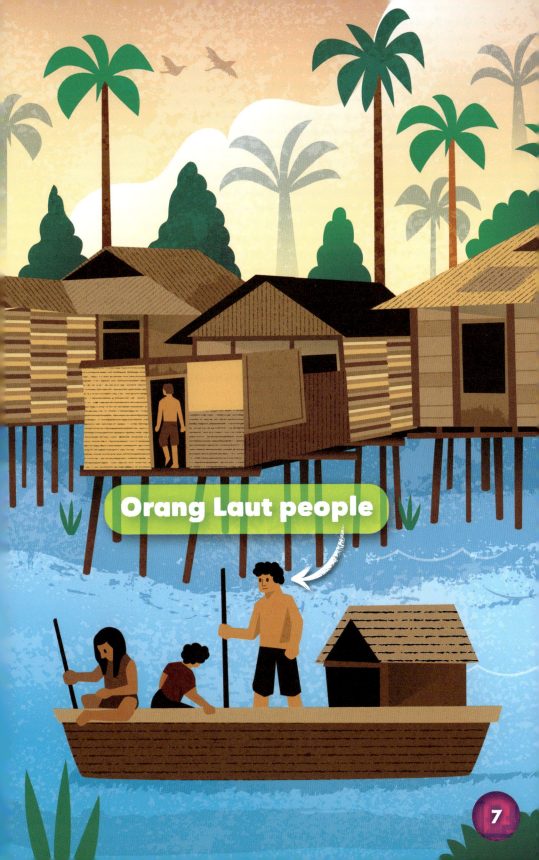

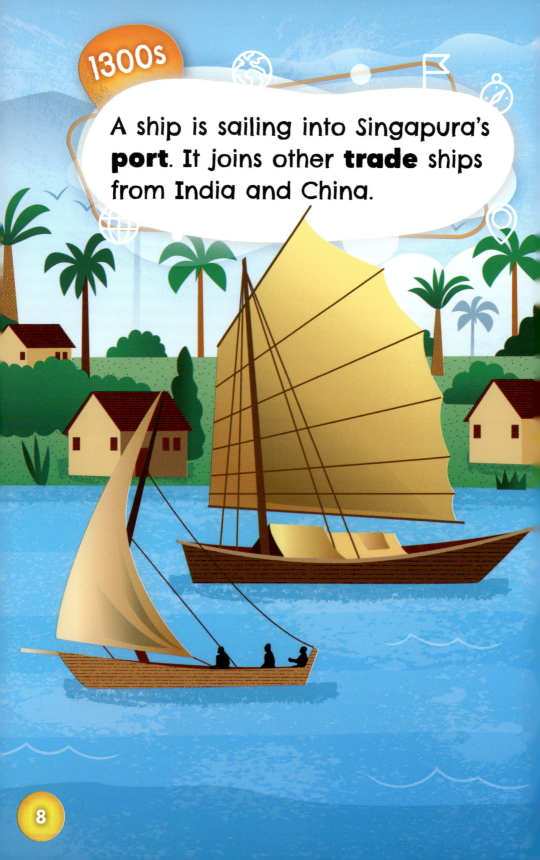

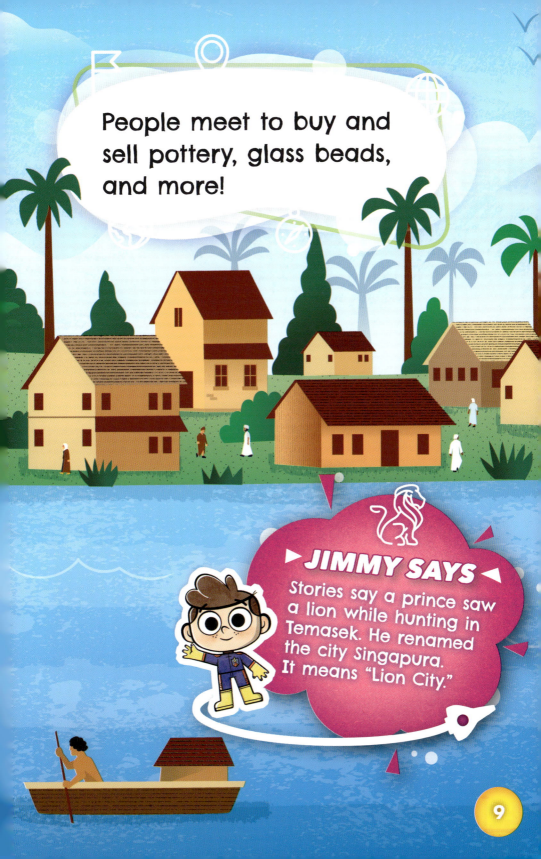

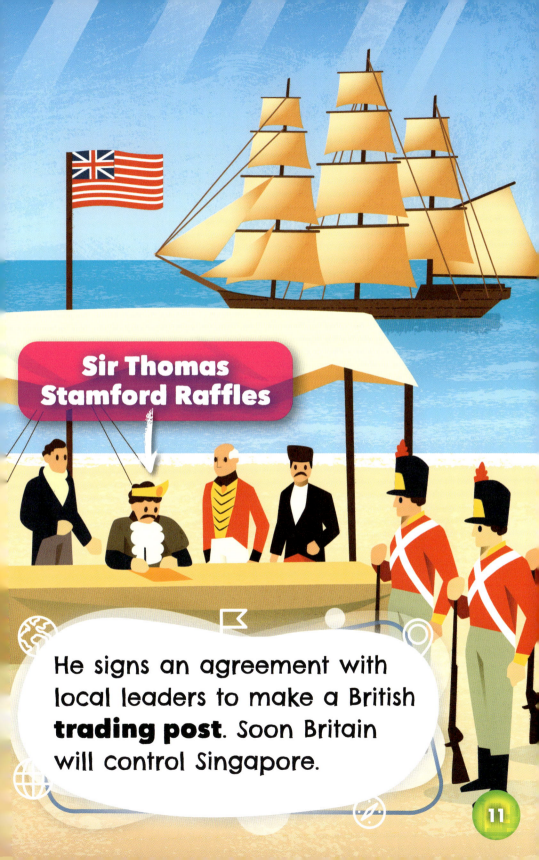

late 1944

World War II has reached Singapore. Japan now controls the city. People hope for change.

U.S. aircraft drop bombs on the docks. Will this help free the city from Japan?

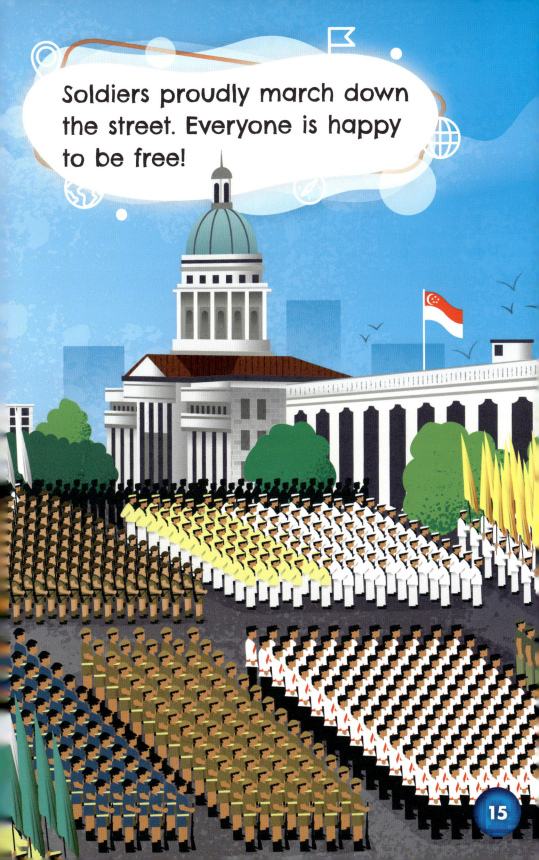

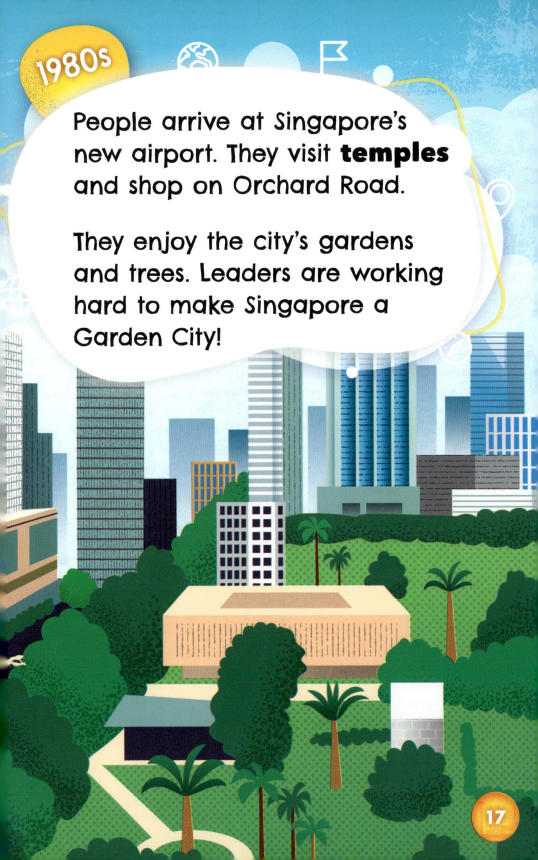

1980s

People arrive at Singapore's new airport. They visit **temples** and shop on Orchard Road.

They enjoy the city's gardens and trees. Leaders are working hard to make Singapore a Garden City!

2012

People walk through Gardens by the **Bay** as the sun goes down.

The Supertrees begin to glow. Music fills the air. It is magical!

The City Today

today

Visitors enjoy Singapore's many buildings covered in plants. They check out museums and parks.

Singapore's history has made it the important port city it is today!

Singapore Timeline

1200s: The Orang Laut people call Temasek home

1300s: Singapura is an important trading post between India and China

1819: Singapore becomes a British trading post

late 1944: The U.S. Army drops bombs on Japanese-controlled Singapore during World War II

1966: The first National Day Parade takes place in Singapore

1980s: Leaders work to make Singapore a Garden City

2012: Gardens by the Bay opens

Glossary

bay–a small area filled with ocean water

city-state–a self-governing city and its surrounding area

culture–the beliefs, arts, and ways of life in a place or society

foraging–searching for food

mangroves–groups of trees and shrubs that grow along coastlines

port–a place where ships load and unload their containers

temples–buildings used for worship

trade–related to the buying and selling of goods

trading post–a place far from cities or towns where goods and services can be traded

World War II–the war fought from 1939 to 1945 that involved many countries

To Learn More

AT THE LIBRARY

Greathead, Helen. *Singapore City Trails*. Oakland, Calif.: Lonely Planet Global Limited, 2018.

Klepeis, Alicia Z. *Singapore*. New York, N.Y.: Cavendish Square, 2019.

Leaf, Christina. *Tokyo*. Minneapolis, Minn.: Bellwether Media, 2024.

ON THE WEB

FACTSURFER

Factsurfer.com gives you a safe, fun way to find more information.

1. Go to www.factsurfer.com.

2. Enter "Singapore" into the search box and click 🔍.

3. Select your book cover to see a list of related content.

BEYOND THE MISSION

› WHAT FACT FROM THE BOOK DID YOU THINK WAS THE MOST INTERESTING?

› WHICH POINT IN SINGAPORE'S HISTORY WOULD YOU LIKE TO VISIT? WHY?

› DESIGN A GARDEN FOR SINGAPORE. WHAT PLANTS WOULD YOU INCLUDE? DRAW A PICTURE.

Index

airport, 17
Britain, 11
British East India
  Company, 10
culture, 6
gardens, 4, 17
Gardens by the Bay, 18
Japan, 13
Malaysia, 14
museums, 20
name, 6, 9
National Day Parade, 14
Orang Laut, 6, 7
Orchard Road, 16, 17
parks, 20
people, 4, 6, 7, 9, 13, 17, 18, 19
port, 8, 20
Stamford Raffles,
  Thomas, 10, 11
Supertrees, 18, 19
Temasek, 6, 9
temples, 17
timeline, 21
trade, 8, 11
World War II, 13